Dear Good
Naked
Morning

Dear Good
Naked
Morning

RUTH L.
SCHWARTZ

Autumn House
Press

PITTSBURGH

The image on the cover is a detail of a mola, at approximately half actual size.

"Mola is the Kuna Indian word for blouse, but the term mola has come to mean the elaborate embroidered panels that make up the front and back of a Kuna woman's blouse. The Kuna Indians are the native people who live on small coral islands in the San Blas Archipelago along the Atlantic coast of Panama and Colombia. Molas are collected as folk art and can be viewed at some of the finest museums in the world like the Smithsonian in Washington, DC." (from sciencejoywagon.com/kwirt/mola/molas.htm)

"Molas, with their multiple layers of meaning, give us insights into what the Kuna value, what they think, and how they feel; for virtually everything—from spaceships to squirrels to earthquakes—is reinterpreted by women in their own terms." (from molamarket.com)

Text and cover design: Kathy Boykowycz

Autumn House Press Staff
Executive Director: Michael Simms
Director of Development: Susan Hutton
Community Outreach Director: Michael Wurster
Assistant Editor: Jack Wolford
Editorial Consultant: Eva Simms
Media Consultant: Jan Beatty
Marketing Consultant: Matt Hamman

ISBN: 1-932870-03-2
Library of Congress Control Number: 2004113776

Printed in the U.S.A. by Thomson-Shore of Dexter, Michigan
All Autumn House books are printed on acid-free paper and meet the international standards of permanent books intended for purchase by libraries.

Does the earth gravitate? Does not all matter, aching, attract all matter?

So the body of me to all I meet or know.

Walt Whitman, "I Am He That Aches With Love,"
from *Body of Adam*

CONTENTS

THE AUTUMN HOUSE POETRY SERIES

Michael Simms, editor

DEDICATION AND THANKS

The writing of this book preceded, prepared me for, and ushered me into a period of profound transformation. For her pivotal role in that process, I dedicate this book to Isa Gucciardi of the Anam.Cara Foundation.

There are a number of people whose presence is strongly felt in these poems; in particular, for all they've taught me about love and pain, I thank Kim Rose Korkan, Marianne Dresser, Anna Benassi and Rebecca Nobel Aguirre. Julia B. Levine and Alison Luterman supported and accompanied me throughout, and the opening lines of "Green Fuse" are Julia's, as are the italicized lines in "December 31." Witting and unwitting contributions were made by Sarah Murray, Molly Fisk, John Donoghue, Natalie Bradley, Bodhi, and many musicians whose names I never knew. Gailyn Thomas told me about Vermont's "mud season," and Don Morrill suggested to me that we need the intractable. Don also provided helpful critiques of "Green Fuse" and other poems, as did Kim Rosen, Kim Addonizio and Stacey Waite. And Kim Rosen renewed my faith in poetry as a tool of transformation—and also inspired me to experiment with form.

I wrote most of these poems while teaching at California State University-Fresno, and I am grateful for the contributions my colleagues, students and the California highways made to my poetic life. And of course my profound appreciation goes out, always, to the birds, cows, cats, dogs, insects, and all my other creature-teachers.

ACKNOWLEDGMENTS OF PREVIOUS PUBLICATION

"Sex," *Runes: The Mystery Issue*, 2002
"Letter from Ellis Pond," *Mid-American Review*, 2002
"Highway Five Love Poem," *Kalliope*, 2003
"Palimpsest," "Ceremony," "Photograph of the Child," "Perseid," "December 31,"
    In The Grove, 2003
"Music for Guitar and Stone," *Tampa Review*, 2002
"Tangerine," *Crab Orchard Review*, 2003
Section 5 of "Letters Addressed to Love," *The Sun*, 2002

I

COME WITH ME

Come with me up to the rim of the city, the ridge of hill
which waits for us, forbidding, forgiving, implacable,
its naked bruises dry as stones in summer wet as soup of mud
in winter, forcing our feet up through rungs of bone,
sucking them down like a last proposal – saying
There is no other world
for us to love, only this one,
fantastic disaster –
where vultures stand beside the fallen
head of deer as at the head
of some great table, one by one waiting their turn
to sip the nectar of the eye.

The nectar of the I:

above the Eladio's Bail Bond billboard, its grinning
promises, its opened metal doors – *Lo Sacamos
Del Bote Hoy.* Above the city storefront churches, *Temple of Love*
boarded and sealed, *Temple of The Word,*
the cars hiked up on rusted wheels in shaggy driveways,
the slinking cats with oil-dragged tails, who cry and cry
for food, but run when we come near –

Where is my life?

Is it in Socios Garage, grimy, unheated, impatient as tires are
levered onto my car, or is it in the five-week-old pit bull
I hold while I wait, because it's there, because it shakes
with cold or fear, groans like a dying man until I wrap my scarf
around the tremble, and it rests? Is it in the dog outside, already
trained and chained, the years of meanness layered onto him, the heart
which doesn't speak, but snarls? Or in what hasn't happened yet?
And where does it go when I leave, the puppy whimpers back to its kicked
cardboard, when I drive away?

Come with me like the junkie pounding
on the window of the pickup,
If you love me, open the door.
If you love me, open the door.
If you ever loved me, open the goddamned door –

until I think she must be right, the door itself is damned.

Now she screams off down the street,
staggers, crumples to the curb.
The truck speeds through the light, swerves, backs up.

Sometimes that's all I want: to love you,
whoever you are.

Below us the ruthlessly quarried water,
two deer nosing their way to the far shore
to drink.

It's spring; even the dumpsters gleam.
A woman climbs inside and digs,
uncovering a whole Big Mac, still wrapped;
I watch her hand it to her man
the way a bride forks cake into the mouth
of her new husband, in the kind of light which lives
between two faces, and refuses nothing.

PHOTOGRAPH OF THE CHILD

for my sister

Your mouth is open as a world
The skin on your arms is soft as the flowering world
You're jumping barefoot in the grass, no one is
stopping you; no one and nothing has destroyed you yet
Your skinny little belly, its navel an off-center planet
Your shorts bunched-up, your little knees uneven with the jump
Only your toes are touching, your heels have already leapt
I will frame you like this forever before and after
I abandon you
And who's alive who doesn't remember
floating, at least once, above the ordinary street?
And who's never made a promise they couldn't keep?

LETTER FROM ELLIS POND

for Kim

I've come here to let the grief scour me,
I mean, to stop pretending I have another choice.
I hold myself as tenderly
as a sack full of fresh eggs.
I take this tenderness into the world,
which does not need it, but receives it
like a rock ground smooth by water.
I stand with my feet in the tiny stream
and watch a bird bow down a single
tasseled grass-blade with its small weight,
and watch the velvet dragonflies
alight on, ascend from the watercress'
lustrous green leaves.
There is no other way for me to mourn
your loss, by which I mean no other way
to celebrate your gift to me, by which I mean
this isn't about what I mean, this is about what *is* –
and the abundance of it, and the raw unfinished
sheen of it,
and the slender-bodied fish
who carry the river inside them, bubbled
mouth to fin – I mean I have never seen a more beautiful
world than the one you left me in,
the gift inextricable now from the loss,
the dragonflies drawing shut
their doubled wings.
I walk like a giant in this stream,
my pants rolled up, my sandals ruined,
as the fish go on moving like shadows of fish,
fierce confetti changing direction, saying in their swish
nothing but this, nothing but this –

and the roots of everything hold me in place,
and the current tugs me forward,
and the grasses bow down, not for me, not
in spite of me,
and a single purple thistle
bends its fragrant head
as if to drink.
All right then, I admit, the grief and love are one,
the warp and woof are one, the fleck and stroke, the
strobe and jut are one,
the world in all its gorgeous indifference, the heart
leaking yolk from its broken shell,
the choices made, unmade, unborn and borne
aloft like milkweed, the sky full of parachute seeds –

SEX

It's the church of pleasure and sorrow.
All its intricate windows have been smashed.
It holds the places where the stars
opened inside us, blood on shattered glass.
It holds the light between us,
brighter than anything –
except for the equal measure of darkness,
sealed inside our bodies,

which eclipses it.
O stubborn animal, celestial, transforming.
O spasm which loves nothing but itself,
aware of nothing but itself, grateful to nothing.
O firefly which asks, What do you most want?
as it sputters out.

WORDS

Comfort me, please, by singing

in some language I don't understand.
I want your words, but not to have to pretend
I know what they mean.

Today the sky has that held-back brightness
which makes me think of Puerto Rico; I was fifteen,
walking alone, early, in the sticky air,
and got a ride with a guy in a truck
who told me he'd like to eat me out
right there in the cab.
But when I said *I don't think so*, he shrugged,
not unfriendly, and took me
where I was going.

Words did a good enough job then.

They mostly fail when you love someone.

 I remember weeks with a woman
I can't speak to now,
and how the loving sparked and crackled,
swung and stretched and shone us open; sometimes,
in those hours of joy and touch,
we'd look at each other and say, *You're, you're –*

and find no way to finish the thought
except when one of us once stumbled onto,
        You're God –

        though even that seemed just to hint at
more we couldn't say.

Later we stood as far apart
as egrets
in a flooded field, and words

were all we had to send
across the space and time between us –
sullen, roaring,
stubborn, weeping,
sorry, sorry words.

Words are even worse when you're smart,
and know more of them –

for instance, when you're not just smart, you're *articulate* –

sometimes then you really get fooled
into thinking you can *say* it –
whatever it is.

Just now I saw 10,000 blackbirds
making a single shape like smoke, if smoke
could pour so many bodies,
ribbon-skitter-silver-flitter,
into one;
I could spend the rest of my life
trying to describe
the way they spoke to the air, and
each other,
the way they were and were not
a single bird –

PALIMPSEST

Down here at the raggedy edge of the shore –
        There are people who never leave when they leave us,
no beach, only an endless roil of waves
        people who live inside us like swimmers, moving
shoving each other for space –
        the arms they used to hold us, or push us away –
everybody's looking for something:
        that stroke which overflows the heart,
pigeons for crumbs, gulls for rotten fish,
        then drains, then fills. Who can blame us
the water for something else it can wet.
        for drinking it up? Who can abandon desire?
How fine it would be, you think, to love your life:
        We need the intractable, I tell you,
to love the body of absence
        to open us; we need its shadows to serve us
in your body.
        by falling away.

THE LOST AND PHYSICAL WORLD

Where you walked *I Love You* with your feet, dragging the words
through a drift of dunes –

and redwings hidden in the reeds
thrummed like an orchestra of hearts,

and cormorants held out their faithful arms.
The stalk of your neck was so tender, I bruised it,
kissing you.

There was a woman
sculpted nude in sand –

voluptuous, her breasts of sand,
nipples of sand pinched into small hard cones.

We watched a toddler, clumsy on his feet,
maybe two years old,

break from his parents, stumble joyfully to her,
to take those nipples between his fingers –

It was only later I thought, How grieved he must have been.

TREES IN WIND

How sure they are, the trees in wind,
gangly, manic, drugged, exuberant; rustling,
reckless, lost; wringing a thousand hands
over a thousand graves; placing long fingers
to long lips, saying Hush, all is not lost
that you think is lost; saying There are costs
you have not yet paid. They know more than you
want to know, you who want to know

everything. They know more than that and aim
to tell it all night long, in song you can't repeat
or translate; Don't forget, they say, and pray, equally
to the gods of wind and ground; chance and purpose;
air and failure; gods of all things fallen, their limbs
block the way, arrow toward the way.

LOVE POEM FOR THE PAST

Because your stories flare open like bullets,
Because you drink like your father, betray like your mother,
Because you still attack as you were attacked,

Because you shot the soft brown birds, because he gave you the gun,
    and he was your father,
Because you want to kill him for that, to kill the place he lives in you,
    to break his human neck,
Because I kiss your human neck, your downy shoulder-blades,
    charred stubs of wings.

                      Why have we been brought here? the music asks,
but it taps a cymbal as it asks, plays a little riff on the asking, and I know
someone somewhere is slowly dancing, not to answer, but only to honor the
question. The music shrugs and goes on playing, shrugs and shivers a little,
swings and sways a little in its play. It brought us here and goes on bringing –
such faith in it, such opened body of sound.

Each note is a stone laid down; the stones make a path.
Each path is made of many stones, and leads nowhere.
But there is joy in stones which follow each other like this;
joy in notes which coax and stroke
and hope and pluck such music from their veins.

DECEMBER 31

for Julia

It's true, the black cows
stand as mute as stone
through the flooding rain –
and when it stops, it's true, they bend
again to the rapacious
greenness of the earth.

This morning the dock has risen
high as it can go.
There are no stairs to descend; the water
has come up to meet you.
Why stand at the edge
with arms and legs spread,
why say, This is the soul
and the narrow rotted swaying planks
you walked to get here are the body;
why say, this last day of the year,
Today the soul does not wish
to leave the body.
Today it can't think of anywhere else
it would rather be.

Why pretend a choice
between despair and grace?

Even the worms inside the branches
carve a kind of art
out of their endless hunger.

Even the vulture holds itself in place
in sky, in moving air.
Its wings are made
to bear such hovering.

MUD SEASON

In Vermont, the season between Winter and Spring

God made the mud and now she has to crawl in it.
She's not the only one.
Dolores, for example, with her matted hair, her pushed-up breasts,
pills to take the fear away, men who pay her by the hour:
God on her belly in the muck. God on her knees.
When nothing has yet become what it will become,
when no astonishment of green has yet unfurled,
when pain feels larger than our lives – nothing
has yet become what it will become.
Who wouldn't choose a different season, if they had a choice?
I lie down in the dark and listen to my heart:
that circling helix in the chest.
Apart from me, apart from love, apart from
even the question of love: original, pulsing, unscarred.

VERSIONS OF GHALIB:
GHAZAL I

Ghalib was a 19th-century Urdu poet. These versions were developed from the prose translations provided by Aijaz Ahmad in *Ghazals of Ghalib* (Columbia University Press, 1971). Numbering corresponds to the numbers used in that volume.

i

Everything sings, in each moment, a song – and is,
in the very next moment, unsung.

It's no use being a mirror which sees both sides;
both sides are wrong.

What you claim to know will fail you; so will
what you venerate. Drink up. Refill your cup.

Deliberately love kicks up dust
to irritate the eye between two worlds.

ii

Each song loves and hates itself.
If there's a mirror which tells the difference, don't look.

Forget what you know; don't bother to believe.
Not-knowing is the only cup which can hold the world.

Where love has been and gone, the world grows honest.
Each thing sings: *I am essential. I do not exist.*

All you think you know is wrong. So is all you worship.
No matter how much you drink, there's more in the cup.

iii

Praise the futility of song. Accept that the shine in the mirror
is wrong. You are not important.

What's a mirror, anyway? Who looks back from that bright glass?
It's love again, come to save us, or drive us mad.

The more you know, the less you see;
faith can't be drunk, though it fills your cup.

Love's like a dust which settles on all things
and clings like skin. Even the sky bows down to it.

GHAZAL II

Hard things were never meant to be easy.
The difficult would lose its mind if given too much grace.

Even humans can never become fully human.
It wouldn't be human to go just so far, and not yearn to go farther.

Love demands to be seen; it insists that we polish the mirror.
What we don't see is that this polishing *is* love.

We think we'll die of so much desire;
then love lights up like a hundred orchards in bloom.

After it kills us, it swears it won't hurt us again.
The recanting of the song is as beautiful as the singing.

GHAZAL V

The drop of water can't truly live until it drowns in the river.
The pain which can't be borne will bear us away on its back.

When we're weakened enough by tears, they dry into breath.
So water turns into air; so what we are can transform.

After the falling of so much rain, the clear sky is a kind of death.
It's like that with our weeping, too, and the joy that follows.

The polished side of the mirror is a miracle to us;
but look, the mossy side is equally miraculous.

There's always another blooming rose, another life to witness, Ghalib!
No matter what the world looks like, continue to look.

GRASS

Yesterday, and the day before that,
the cows ate grass.
Tomorrow, and the next, and every day after that,
the cows will eat grass.
They'll eat until they can't stand up,
and even then, collapsed upon the earth in their last hours,
if they can reach it with their mouths, they'll eat grass.
They'll eat until they've eaten it all, until there are only
a few stray blades
halfway buried under boulders – then
they'll nudge aside the boulders
with their large and knowing lips,
and eat that grass, too.
Only the smallest calves, today,
the ones no bigger than dogs, are lying down.
They gaze out onto the landscape like dreamers:
the sky marbled with fatty clouds;
the cherry trees beginning to leaf;
the first few poppies, unfurling their cadmium banners;
the fences making some things possible, and others difficult;
the shadows falling from, and following, each thing;
and the world seems so strange, so common and wondrous
at once, that the calves ask the cows eating grass,
Is this all there is?
And the answer comes back from mouths full of grass:
This is all there is.

HIGHWAY FIVE LOVE POEM

for Anna

This is a love poem for all the tomatoes
spread out in the fields along Highway Five,
their gleaming green and ruddy faces like a thousand
moons prostrate in praise of sun.
And for every curd of cloud,
clotted cream of cloud spooned briskly
by an unseen hand into the great blue bowl,
then out again, into a greedy mouth.
Cotton baled up beside the road,
altars to the patron saint of dryer lint.
Moist fudge of freshly-planted dirt.
Shaggy neglected savage grasses
bent into the wind's designs.
Sheep scattered over the landscape like fuzzy confetti,
or herded into stubbled funnels, moving like rough water
toward its secret source.
Egrets praying in the fields like
white-cloaked priests.
A dozen wise and ponderous cows
suddenly spurred to run, to gallop, even,
down a flank of hill.
Horses for sale, goats for sale, nopales for sale, orange groves for sale,
topless trailers carrying horses,
manes as loose and lovely as tomorrow in our mouths,
and now a giant pig, jostling majestic in the open
bed of a red pickup,

and now a fawn-colored coyote
framed between the startled fruit trees
who looks directly at me before loping back
into the world he owns.
Even the bits of trash are alive,
and chase each other in the wind, and show their underwear.
Even the sparrows hop like the spirit,
sustain themselves on invisible specks,
flutter and plummet, rise straight up like God.

TANGERINE

It was a flower once, it was one of a billion flowers
whose perfume broke through closed car windows,
forced a blessing on their drivers;
then what stayed behind grew swollen, as we do;
grew juice instead of tears, and small hard sour seeds,
each one bitter, as we are, and filled with possibility.
Now a hole opens up in its skin, where it was torn from the
branch; ripeness can't stop itself, breathes out;
we can't stop it either. We breathe in.

WALKING IN WINTER

1

The rains have made the earth more tractable.
It sticks to our shoes like clay, like shit,
like the deepest workings of the body; spatters up our legs.

The dog alive with new scents, redemption
of drizzle instead of downpour,
runs with all her lean muscle
ahead and back,

gallops toward the life which might be
hidden and might run from her;
stops, sometimes, to stalk it instead,
one foreleg raised with ancient trembling –

the gophers' tunnels extend underground
like veins branched through the body of earth –

then digs not only with paws
but with muzzle,
mouthing the mud in a glory of digging; ripping it
to sparks, to tiny waterfalls; spraying it around like sperm, crazed
with joy and will, delirious
with purpose.

2

There's a trick to wanting what we want,
then letting go of it –
we haven't learned it yet.
Longing is a boat
which carries us for miles –

till it grows tired, and tiresome,
ties itself in riverweeds,
floats as long as it can
and then goes under.

We've come to the ribs of the world,
the bones in its bony hands.

Water runs through every one of them.

The ground sucks up at us like someone
who's too weak to hold a cup;
who's grabbed a straw

and drinks. And will survive.

Rain quivers on the branches:
tiny fruit.

3

The dry used-up worn-out grass
stands stiff and still, each blade
a tall dead sentry; and the new young hopeful grass

grows underneath, between, around, in spite of
everything. I can't help loving life
as metaphor,
though I also love it as itself:

the jelly-bodied newts, for instance,
awkward, ponderous,
crab-walking, back legs touching front,
each step
        half a loss.

They've come to worship the flooded world.

They can't move fast, but they keep moving.

I lift one into my palm, and it keeps moving.

                     Parkridge Trail, Oakland

CEREMONY

The room is dark but light burns in the mouths and in the cunts,
light pulses in the labyrinths of belly, in the fingertips.
As if it carried seeds which need to plant themselves,
light goes on trying to make its way out –
searching out the soil which lives
inside the pleasure of the other,
the water of her voice turning liquid,
the sun of her body thrusting upward. There is a goodness in this
and a strangeness, tilling the unknown other so closely,
the fingers thinking *Love*, the mind remembering *Not yet*,
reminding itself *Maybe never*, while the body says more softly,

                                                              Love –

inside the thrumming of nipples and cunt, heart and pulse,
the sucking harder and harder at sweetness, the wisdom of flesh.

FIFTH STREET LOVE POEM

1

There is a piano in the street.
There is a man in white shirt and black blazer.
He wears white gloves on his hands, saluting the street air.
He plays as if our lives are beginning.
He plays against the sunset bubble
in each parking meter: Time Expired.

There is a man with a long beard:
colors of street and snow mixed together,
colors of earth and fire.
He is wearing a blue miniskirt.
His legs and feet are bare.
His calves are taut with muscle,
thick with hair,
animal, intelligent; rippling as he lifts each foot,
slow as prayer, then sets it down again.
He is checking the coin return slots
of the public telephones,
thoughtfully he feels inside each one
for the coins which aren't there –
and then moves on, his bare toes curling
over and into the street
as if it were sand, and could give way,
even a little bit, beneath him.
He looks like the first man
walking on the first earth,
feeling with his feet for the footholds,
the thresholds, the intimate designs.

2

Your fingers stroking the base of my spine, and the slow
sweat that starts there, and your knowledge of it.
Your lips like the rounded lip of the water
added drop by drop into a full cup.

Band of light at grey horizon:
doubled and redoubled, tripled, trebled light.
Raindrops massed on windshield glass:
shards of some great thing that shattered whole.

Afterward, at Our Lady of Lourdes,
A flame of love for every intention,
hundreds of candles flickering
in cement-block rooms,
we look down at our hands and see them
capable as anyone's,
we see in the glass case the cast-off
evidence of miracles:
crutches, braces, wheelchair spokes,
oaths of gratitude and praise.

So much we can't hold
still shudders close to us.
A blind boy on the curb, his dog,
the taut loveliness of the leather strap –
the clean pull, life against life,
life enjoined to life – as the dog moves forward
into the street, and the boy follows.

3

The music never stops. It's never the wrong life.
The mushrooms poke their hard-boiled heads
through the lip of grass,
the grass breaks through the black smoothed-over
crusted grief of street,
the lovers tug each others' arms
like surgeons' guidewires, mountain climbers' ropes.
Inside our bodies, something always waits
to disappear, or burn, or startle us with bloom.

The moon rises high, partial and wise,
glowing like something
that wants to save us –
yet it does nothing but cast light.
From every tree the cicadas insist,
as if the combined sum of their voices,
round as bicycle chains,
could lift the legs of the dead onto pedals
and ride them away.

4

Okay, I tell the trees, I want the leaves;
I want the beetles
which devour the leaves.
I say: I will take this leaf,
eaten already to lace, as the whole leaf.
I will take it as evidence:
a structure of cells holds us together,
the body is a skein
for all the shades of green,
a cup to catch the apple-cider light
when someone pours it down.

Okay, I tell the cars,
whooshing by like waves on speed:
I love each one of you.
Fleeting speedy ghosts of proof, evidence
of presence and absence,
approach, arrival and departure, imminent, unstoppable –

and music still the only thing which hears us,
takes us in, and heals us into notes.
The music never stops. It's never the wrong life,
though so often it seems to be.
I still don't know what it would mean
to lay down all my weapons and love you.
If I did, then
          what wouldn't I love?

MUSIC FOR GUITAR AND STONE

In music I can love the small failures,
the ones which show how difficult it is:
the young guitarist's fingers slipping,
for an instant, from their climb of chords.
He sits alone on the stage, bright light,
one leg wedged up on a step, his raised knee
round and tender, and the notes like birds
from a vanishing flock, each one more exquisite and lonely;
the fingers part of the hand, yet separate from the hand,
each living muscle married to the whole.
In life the failures feel like they'll kill me,
or you will, or we'll kill each other;
it's so hard to feel the music
moving through us, the larger patterns
of river and mountain, where damage is not separate
from creation, transformation;
where every mistake we make can wash
smooth and clean as stones in water,
then land on shore, then be thrown in again.
I want to sleep, like a stone, for a thousand years.
I want to wake with creatures traced smooth on my skin.
I want to forget I loved you and failed you
as you failed and loved me too, in the lengthy, painful
evolution of our kind; I want to sleep
for a thousand years, then wake up in some other world
where failure is part of the music, and seen
to make it more beautiful; where the fingers
forgive each other; where we can sit naked again
at the window, watch the notes fly by like birds
who have finally found their way home.

PERSEID

August meteor shower

While they're here I hold them
like my breath. They deepen the sky
like blood in my body, I'm glad to offer
my body like this – a small craft
over fields of water,
where light can fall, be lost, be caught,
be held.
I'm naked in my chair,
facing the window.
If I were outside I'd want to look up
and see someone naked in every window.
I think we need
the difficult river, we need the absence of tenderness
so love can come like shooting stars
if it comes.

LETTERS ADDRESSED TO LOVE

1

Dear good naked morning,
I miss you.

My ferocious perfume.
My green-melon joy.

Night too has bone,
my lips did fly.

Prisoner, I linger near you.
The movements which might save us

are so small.

2

Out on the highway, near the half-built Burger King,
a great blue heron stalks leftover marsh.
Steps like a stilt-walker, deliberate,
over plywood, nails.
Crooking his ancient neck, he looks like
something from another world –
which, in fact, he is.
It doesn't matter; what sustains him
is simple enough. Need not be beautiful.

3

Now the dark raven, cloaked in shine,
holds the body of a smaller bird
against a rim of stone.

Each sensation
an explosion.
Every nerve and synapse
firing like a gun.

With his surgeon beak, he tears
the flesh and eats.

4

Two pigeons do their sidewalk dance. The male
hops on top, spreads his hallelujah tail,
shudders, chortles off again. And
the magnolia, blowzy with flower,
drunk and rich and thick with flower, blooming
that bloom none of us can stop, swaying, unashamed,

lowers its full branches to the curb
in a kind of bow.

5

Forgiveness circles us. The words we speak are birds:

sometimes descending from the tops of trees
to bathe in the water left over in gutters,
diamonds splashing off their shoulders –

sometimes coming close enough to lay their beaks
against our naked palms.

TENER

I remember the note in which I told you our love had come to feel *untenable* to me. Untenable: it comes from the same Latin root as the Spanish *tener*, to have. *Tengo*: I have. *Tendré*: I will have. *Tuve*: I had. It's profoundly irregular.

I watch two spiders on a trellis, rising and falling on their own threads. I listen to voices behind me, murmurs too soft to have meaning, and then the scraping of chairs on cement. The lake is calm and still, the boaters have gone home, the clouds mount between and behind the mountains, waiting to be subsumed by the body of night. A small tree trembles a little, down by the water.

I remember how hard I wanted. How hard you wanted. How hard that hardness was between us, like a rib or shin.

The hammock sways in the late breeze; its shadows climb the railing a little, then stop to consider the mixing of light into dark. Each leaf on the tree above it has a shadow leaf, a twin, a doppelganger, an alternate self – which is, in this moment, alive on the wood, and held and swaying a little. Each one looks something like a heart, pinched between two fingers and made to dance.

There wasn't love to be mined from that place, that hard bone. But at times a bird swooped from one chest into the other's flesh.

Underneath what I wanted then is a more faithful layer of want, steady, sustaining: a bridge. One day, naked alone in bed, I feel it. Palm on my own animal belly, as if there were something for me to glean from myself. Beneath the lake are bricks from an abandoned city. What's left under the bricks is skin, and everything it knew before the flood.

SPRINGTIME IN THE CENTRAL VALLEY

Even the oldest trees are blooming, limbs growing down
instead of up, producing a personal halo of fallen petals.
Even the fat sheep bloom in the fields, their faces thick with unshorn wool,
their coats springy as lettuces.
Even the tractors bloom, pledged to churning dirt;
the dented pickup in the grove, delirious with oranges;
the waxy schoolbus, crayon-yellow,
child in each window, laughing like a star.
Even the drivers of the cars open their pink mouths.
The cows are blooming: great brown roses,
egrets white like thorns between them.
Animals die and bloom on the roads,
revealing the plump burst plums of their organs;
the living feed among the dead,
the living feed *upon* the dead:
murmuring flashing scatter of flies,
jeweled and diligent.
Everything is perfect, each thing seems to say
with dead or living beak, or finely jointed legs,
intricate bristles of tail, or sturdy teeth.
The golden eagle says it from a branch,
blurting out a proud white squirt of shit.
The milkweed seed with its slim brown propeller
and dozens of filaments waving like arms.
The silvery-snow-rust-dusted coats
of the prairie dogs, and the fox who hunts them.
Everything says it, sighs it, chirps it,
clicks and whistles, rustles, wrests it into form,
flaps and swoops and coos and hums it into form,
squawks or caws or snorts it out, slimes it

into algae-puddles, flutters into wings,
perches, dips, drips and sails,
trails a wake like a vein through the water,
nervy, improbable.
Marry me over and over, says the world,
offering sun on our shoulders, a mantle, a cloak of hands.

GREEN FUSE

The force that through the green fuse drives the flower
Drives my green age...

Dylan Thomas

i

There's so much death out here, you say.
That's why I like it.

Here in front of us, a bloated frog,
belly swollen as a sunflower –
dead thing
                  covered with life, swarming with it:
broken dotted lines of ants, daring miners dipping,
gleaning what they can;
steady music of the flies
who come to glitter, bejewel
with their bodies, praise with their
opening closing wings – all this
beautiful death...

The rocks on this beach cut our feet –
without malice,
without capacity for malice.
Tough and porous, ancient hardened ash.
The small bone stars of barnacles
attach themselves, grow outward, thrive.
The mussels, bruise-colored valves of wing and heart,
clamp tight, and live.

There's so much death out here, you say.

It's true, the beach is black and blue
with decimated hearts:
shells emptied of what needed them,
crouched on the sand like hands
cut off in prayer.
I want you to know, I don't hold this against you,

though sometimes I can't hold it any more
against myself,
sometimes the goddamned heart beats
out of its cage,
the halves split apart with a little crack,
the cellular glue of the hinge gives way.

(What does it matter if, after all,
we don't get what we think we want?
Aren't we, anyway, always hollow
and full, in the same moment?
Aren't we alive in the yearning,
in the appetite?)

ii

Quiet between us, after weeks of blame,
both of us in our corners, snarling, sad
over things we can barely name, yet
fiercely lay claim to, insist upon,
until the words have repeated themselves
so often their tongues are twisted and lost –
the words themselves leave us behind,
leave us lost.
The ridge under the full moon
stretches, glowing silver,
its long seedheaded grasses ruffled like the fur
of some enormous animal; we walk its back,
its haunches, not talking,
not touching, though it wills us to touch.
This world, if it understands anything,
understands failure.
Do you know I love you still?

Do you know this despair
is just the beginning of love?

Somewhere, it's still daylight.
The people we were once
are still alive,
are taking off their clothes and entering
each other, or the lapping water,
while the clouds watch them like cotton
and the sky says nothing.

Love, let us try again,
and, after failing,
try some more.
Let us hold to each other the way the foxtails,
thistles, burrs hold to our shoelaces –
willing themselves to be transported.

iii

Two flies collide in the air, then land separately,
like jewels, on the leaves of the fig.
A mourning dove hoots like a slow sad train.
Men trimming hedges, mowing lawns
grind out a high-pitched song.
The 20-year-olds across the street, the ones with the VW

without a muffler – I curse every time I hear its
stuttered roar – drive up in string bikini tops
and cut-off pants, and the animal in me
notices their bellies, not firm but rounded, and how
the triangles of cloth
shape themselves like hands around each of their breasts.

A scrub jay squawks,
high in a tree.
A courting pigeon puffs his chest,
swells his proudly purple neck.

(I want to love what is given, and crave nothing else.
Why isn't it enough, the way the trees stand firm,
regretting neither dark nor light?
The way the girls across the street
bring blankets onto their lawn, and beer,
and flash their butterfly hands through the late air –
the way their loud car shouts when they turn the key,
joyful, grateful, ravenous –)

The pigeon fans his feathers, drags the ground
with his ballgown train,
urgently unravels the knit stripes
of his wings and tail. He paces, cowers, bends
    this way and that,
hopping toward the one he wants –
there, strutting through leaves in the gutter –

Joy. You won't be beckoned or pursued.
Come and go on your own immutable terms.
Come with touch, slip from touch.
Come in solitude, leave it like a husk.
Make the heart, make every tissue and organ swell
    with common wonder.
Cannot be prohibited. Cannot be kept.

(And here's this fly, rubbing together
first its front limbs, then its rear –
is it grooming? praying? these legs thin as eyelashes,
rear ones reaching up to riffle through its wings,
front ones rippling, almost braiding,

passing a bow over an unseen violin,
playing a piece of soundless music –
and then the rear again, repetitive, consistent,
as if drawing beads down a patient string;
then it sits in repose for a minute, then
starts up again, with new fervor –
and then another, smaller fly lands on the table,
begins the same meticulous performance –)

Nothing is wrong. Light rises in the sky each day
and casts itself on each thing in the garden, each in its hour,
    at its given angle, each for its duration.
Will not be begged to stay a moment longer, or shine
    elsewhere, or to spill its shadow differently.

Dark slides over us.

    iv

The still sadness of the morning, which is also joy.
Gnats hovering like tiny satellites,
then forking figure-eights, then racing scribbles
    through the lightened air.
The spider whose web, woven overnight, has not yet been destroyed
    preens in the center of it:
pearl which made the oyster,
jewel which made the world.
(What we will be
is not determined yet.)
The grass is dead yet tall and holding fast,
each blade, to its pouch of seed,
each seed the promise of a new blade –
life is incipient in death,

contained, safekept, potentiate, implied.
(Love is implied in us. Love is incipient.)

The morning glories open their blue faces.
The tree holds up its basking leaves
like bathers on a beach.

The rosebushes, which bloomed and bloomed
and browned and rotted, held their dead, scattered their dead,
    have made new roses now,
they lift their fragrant bodies toward the sun.

A tiny mantis prays on one of the roses.
Its face is a green pyramid.
Its antennae are black wires beaded with white.
Its rear legs are those of a frog or a dancer,
a champion swimmer whose kicks could carry
    across the Atlantic.
They rise into upside-down Vs, like a child's drawing of mountains.
They grasp, positioning themselves.
Its shorter legs, two on each side,
are covered with fine striations, teeth
from a delicate saw.

The thorns are stony calluses,
petrified kisses with fearsome tips,
tiny profusions of breasts with treacherous nipples –
and it is hard to fathom they are *of* the roses;
they look so alien, they scratch so fast and deep.

The shadows on the tree trunk, the mosaic bark
come and go like hands from loving touch.
(The thorns appear to be not of the rose.)
The mantis, still on the rose, has transferred itself to a petal
on the northern side,

the ends of its long legs bend like feet.
(Sometimes we are sharp thorns to each other.)

The grass is beautiful in death,
each blade in its coiled arch,
its bow of seed,
swaying to its knees, our thighs,
and parted by a hundred winds, combed to a hundred
golden seas – (and your breath
everywhere, and mine) –
they lie down for us.

v

Last night I wanted my lover's tongue
and she gave it to me and we spoke in tongue
and we worshipped in tongue and we writhed in tongue.
Afterward we said to each other –

but no, we said nothing, we could not speak.
Distance between us, and the life which bridges, with its
thin ineffable body, that distance – and what carries us across –

which is only love, and made by love,

made *of* love, borne on currents of love,

over the sharp-edged stones of love.

(The distance, is it also love?
The fear and doubt, in the seeds of their being,
powerfully rising and seeking and clenching –
are they also love?)

You wanted me to fuck you, and I did.
You wanted me to rip you, rake you,
ram you full of everything you'd ever lost,
you wanted me to make it sweet, to
hold my tongue at the same time
against the pink and tender revelations of your flesh,
and I did.

As if I knew what would happen, as if I could
make it happen, as if through me it could
happen, as if the dark light of our bodies, lit
spark of your need in the night bed

        could lead us where it needed us –

the body with its body needs
and body gratefulness,
flame licking up,
flame bearing down –

      vi

The body *wants* to come.

Or no – maybe it's not the body,
it's the orgasm itself
which wants to come:

convulsive scattershot of bloom
pelting itself again and again
into the holy field, the terrible field.
When my friend tells me how, at ten

she was held naked
on a table,
grandfather's hands between her legs
like a cloud of bees –

(Sometimes I think about sleep, how most of us
in our daily bodies
lay ourselves down like the horizon,
shut our tender eyes, and fall. As if a great switch
had been flicked. As if each miracle we are
needed, every day, to let go of the miraculous:
our bodies which know in the daytime to look
both ways, and to differentiate minutely
between the eyes noses and mouths,
of those we love
and the barely-different faces of strangers –
yet daily need to let go into stillness, silence,
no matter what it costs –)

anyway, when she tells me how,
squatting on the kitchen table,
her grandfather's hands on her and in her,

      she came,

I think about that orgasm –

how, for an instant, it must have seemed
it could take in all the shit of the world
and let it out in air and salt,
in breathless, bleaching-spasm light.

      How do we wake and live
      inside these woken bodies?

Our broken lives
aren't wrong or right; that's like calling the wind
wrong or right

                                       as it bends the bodies of trees,

sometimes riffling snuffling through their frondy hair,

or bowing them down in a kind of
slowed Bojangles,

or blowing warm as a lover's mouth
into each cupped and separately trembling leaf,

or snapping in its invisible teeth
entire limbs,
casting them to the ground.
               The wind. We take it into our bodies

until sometimes I think we *are*
 the wind, or the wind is us –
surging as we surge
through the naked world.
(We, after all, are the grandfather
as well as the girl.
Did you think
it was otherwise?
Did you think you were one
and not the other?)

The body, wherever it finds itself,
lays itself down like a horizon,
dies itself open like a volcano.

(In the dream, my friend said, she knew
a story which would save her;

the dream said Don't worry, you'll remember,
but when she woke she didn't remember.
This is my friend who often can't sleep,
who wakes in the dark belly hours of night,
her heart gone wild as trees in storm.
My friend whose body is lush,
demanding as a rainforest,
jungled with life-forms,
profligate with fears.)

(All of our bodies are like that.
Did you think
otherwise, did you think for even a minute
I was not talking about you?)

I have a friend who –
but what does it matter, my friend is only
the *you* whose features I recognize,
whose constellation of eyes, nose, mouth are somehow
separable, for me, from the rest.

(And I could ask, what do we mean
when we say *friend*, when we say *grandfather*?
Do we suppose there are some in our lives
who will not enfold us in cruelty and terror,
and we can name who they are?
Have you ever wanted to break in your hands
the bones of someone you loved?
How many bones have there been,
how many hands?)

Anyway, my friend and I
went walking down at the marina,
where wind and water do what they have to,

whipping into clean peaks
so fierce they startle the eyes
like the blue of flame –

walking and talking, as usual, about love;
my friend thought it was missing from her life.
The trail took us through reeds, where redwings
preened, then rose in red-streaked sparks of black;
where it ended, where nothing was left
to hold us back from water,
we found the glossy pages,
crumpled down between the rocks.
They spoke to us (via captions); they told us,
Tammy wants you to ram your rod down her throat, and
Dora begs, Please slam it up me, baby –

I'm waiting for a way into this poem
the way a man waits for a way into a woman's body,
the way I wait for ways into
your body, or my own,

the way life waits to enter us, and then steam out of us,
enter us, steam free of us –

(And if I love you, and you love me,
and we get drunk on loving each other,
and we spend hours with our mouths on each other,
our bodies losing themselves, which is to say their separateness,
or their illusion of their separateness,
inside the even greater body
of pleasure, which is not ours,
        which belongs to the world –

will anyone be saved?
Will we be saved?)

vii

Little half-moon in the sticky sky,

Little judge and jury of the heat, witness of the night,

Rough-skinned rocky arbiter of tides,

Witness to disturbance, disappearance, to
despair, shining anyway through shifting veils of cloud –

Caster of light, splitter of seams, welder of dark
to dark, stamping light like a rivet
which can't be undone –

I think you look down on us without blame
     or intention,
I think you rise without goodwill
and set without recrimination.
I think you believe in nothing –

but we, because we need to,
believe in you.

(Do You regret us, You who made us?
You who bred our cells into this lineage,
who made us watchful and wasteful,
compassionate and cruel –
You who made everything exist, at the same time,
     in our mortal bodies,
then shook us, stirred us, set us loose
to wreak this love and ruin – ?)

viii

The music swallows us.
It takes us in
on its long tongue.

Longing so much for what has been lost,
and willfully turned away from, and stamped down
into the dirt –
longing for that.

The drummer nodding rocking shrugging
furrowing head rising leaning back –
body jamming with the fine
pressure of his beat,
squint-eyed, open-mouthed –

the making of music
is the making of love.

(And there are those who would do anything for love,
would wring and twist themselves
into any shape at all –
who lose it anyway.
Love doesn't want to be wanted like that.)

The music takes us in
the way love swallows us.

(And there are those who shape their love
around whatever isn't there. Who love best
in absence, where the flame can't overtake them.
Who, in the presence of flame, fight to be free of it.
And then, in darkness, in dim memory light,
call to the fire, yearn and cry and sing,
shape their lives around grief, bend their bodies around air,
dry themselves like leaf-cups, in the form of hands –)

We place our mouths on all the instruments at once.
We mouth the keys the sticks the strings,
the fine long gleaming neck of brass,
the great burnished body of the bass –

We lift our lips, we sip
the gleam of it.

Ix

In this heat, the roses can't help it.
Their swelling pulls the bushes to their knees.
Their fat faces nestle in dirt,
their petals bury the dirt, their fragrance
    blazes, reckless, irrefutable;
they pour and pour themselves out of themselves,
they spend and give, they die and die and die.
I squat beside them, lift their faces to mine.
What's your secret? I ask their silk,
their scarlet golden shamelessness,
and they nod and drowse and spill their scent
and say nothing.

A fly skitters across my pages, lands above the white sea of words.
Ants on the step move north, cross paths
with those ants moving – with equal fury of purpose – south.

Who am I to say what life is worth, what it is for?

x

I open my door to sparrows, pigeons,

robins, scrub jays, crows,

mourning doves, mockingbirds,

dogs, cats, skunks, squirrels,

ants, flies, gnats, bees, cockroaches,

earwigs with their intricate pincers,

enormous junebugs big as doorknobs,

a starry daddy-longlegs resting
on the ceiling, eggs fanned out
around its web,
tiny black sailboats floating on a clear bay –
(when I stand on a chair I see they are not eggs
but baby longlegs, I count fifty-six of them,
orbiting around the great mother planet) –

Brown moths with their wings of filigree and old lace.

White moths, tiny origami flutterings.

Even the mold on an onion, even that.
Its little eyelash crest, fine speckles,
spores of rising black
along the skin's gash,
thin fur of opportunity…

You're still here.

    xi

There's a man at the beach with his car door open,
sitting with one foot on the pavement,
and, between his legs:
a classical guitar.
A metronome on the dashboard,

tapping out the beat.
Also a paper coffee cup, bravely stained.
Yellow sleeves rolled to the elbow,
veins bold in his arms and hands,
his fingers seek and find the notes. Seek and find.
Play certain passages again.
Know there is no failure, simply wait for music –
the ocean in front of him, the entire sea.
(He holds the guitar as I wish to be held.)
His fingers are a flock of birds:
gliding low over the water,
wingtips almost touching it.
His legs are altars,
praising what is difficult.
(It's love he's making, isn't it?)
He plays the music, or, as Spanish says,
he *touches* it –
a hand stroking the air
just above a flame –
resting cool against the forehead
of the broken water.

xii

When the going gets tough, sometimes the tough
get scarred. Sometimes the scars
crisscross the self, until we're swaddled naked
in barbed wire. Until we're
kissed by it: fierce stars grazing the skin.
When the rage comes, when I lay myself down
in front of the train of the rage,
underneath the fear which powers it,

when I lay myself down and cry to you
from the funneled tracks –

       sometimes you slow, even disembark.

       Sometimes the train itself disappears – almost as if
       it had never been.

       Sometimes you jerk it forward, and keep riding.

    xiii

So if we scuff downhill at dusk,

So if the skies up on the ridge
   seem to surround us with their listening,

So if our efforts at speech are clumsy, and
   we make them anyway,

So if a few ripe drupes of berry
   stain my palm, my tongue, my lover's tongue,

So if the world bequeathes itself to us like this,
   that we may eat of it,

So if the world betrothes itself to us like this,

So if, with fragrant dust beneath our feet,
   we pass under two stands of trees,
   one on each side of the path, grown toward each other
   for so many years, they seem to form clasped hands of branches
   over us,

So if, in light of this, in spite/because of this,
   a hush of peace grows palpable in us
   (warm-blooded sensate creatures, after all;
   intelligent and difficult; newly in love,

profoundly weary; certain of almost nothing,
frightened, faithful in spite of ourselves),

So if I tell the details of my story,
in lieu of yours,

So if I assert that it might have been yours,
So if I claim it *was* yours, on some other evening,
path, in some other place,

So if I swear I want what you have always wanted,
and as fiercely,

So if I promise your fears are mine,
our blood is more alike than different,
my heart, transplanted into your chest,
would continue to beat –

I am telling you nothing you did not already know.

xiv

What we think our lives are
is a net not large enough to hold –

Do I really believe that?
Do I really believe we are, all of us,
suspended in some amniotic gel of meaning, purpose
we can't see or feel or smell,
holding us, not safe but –
held?

So the fighting man is floating
So the starved and inarticulate woman is floating
So the man dispossessed by rage, which underneath
is always pain, is floating

So the woman who cannot choose her life
So all of us. So we whose bodies

lie whole and broken on sidewalks. So
all of us. I could say *net,*
I could say *web,* I could say *sea* –

You ask, what if we don't believe?
Isn't belief itself the net, the web, the sea?

But no: when the child covers her eyes,
when she sees nothing but the imprint
of her own pressing fingers,

she thinks you disappear.

What we believe
is never large enough.

You're still here.

xv

It's a window which slides open. One side
open, one side closed: doubled-over glass.
And the fly, complex and delicate,
a tiny engine of will,
skitters and batters again and again
against the closed half.

It swoops around and round my rooms,
it buzzes like a universe,
it won't stop trying, it brings its filigree legs
again and again
to the unyielding glass.

It can see the world out there:
the leafy trees, the matted grass
hiding its luscious dogshit,
            and it means to get there –
everything it wants
is close, so close...

            We watch it.

            As God watches us.

            xvi

The vast grass-covered hill, each stalk bent by wind into
the larger body of the world –
whose instrument is this?
Is it that grass commands the wind, willing or helpless
as a lover's breath?
Is wind an artist, is it God?
If you watch the hillside, how the furrows move –
subtle as lovers' fingertips, encompassing, unstoppable,
relentless, shiftless, wise
as God – and if it makes you weep –
whose instrument are you?
And if you speak to me of this,
and if I stop, behold – to be and hold, to be beholden to,
you and the hillside both –
you an American, also a crumb of history,
you a woman forty-four, also a labyrinth
ageless, ungendered,
you my lover, also a being
furled and hidden from me –

you and this plane of grass-covered land
angled toward sea.
And if I watch and hold and love you both, and
love you all – whose instrument am I?

xvii

This tree is twice my age,
a dozen times my size;
its leaves are visible to me, as my own cells are not.
I want to study it and learn about my life.
Some branches fully leafed, expansive, patient, wise;
some wavering downward, shading themselves and others;
some growing straight, without obstruction,
nothing to keep their bodies separate from the big sky.
And others which are only sticks, where nothing grows.
(Still: nests can be wedged there. Webs strung span to span.)

Are you happy? asks the one I love,
or, more precisely, the one I love now,
and I answer truthfully, *I am.*

(I answer you as well: *I died
without your love. I did not die.*)

The seedy heads of grass-blades
nod and nod.
A million wheatcolored rainbows,
tougher than we ever imagined.
(And if the *you* of this poem keeps changing,

if love holds close a different body
every lifetime, every night,

isn't that what it's for?)

xviii

A bloodstain trickles onto the pavement.
Above us, clouds form themselves
    in the shapes of continents.

The stain fans out at the top, like a limb
    wrested from its socket.
It forks at the bottom, beginning two roads.
Multi-colored grains of stone
    which have been hardened into concrete,
    shine from underneath it –
    blood gnarls over them.

This stain has tributaries, like a river.
It is the color of bricks made liquid,
    then hardened again into brick.
It tells the only story it can, without apology.
It becomes, in this way, a part of the pavement,
    a skin, a life-form of the pavement.

If you revile it
If you lay your body down, and touch your lips to it
If you hose it hard with water, and
    scrub and scrub at it,
it will say nothing.

Oh God, I love you, it won't cry
It's all your fault, neither will it cry

Its color seems to prove something.
The fact of its color, its faithfulness:
indelible, irreducible...

When the wind blows, when dried leaves skitter over it
    as if they were playing Hopscotch, hopping
    here and there on the body of blood,

63

When people walk on it, placing upon it and then removing
   the soles of their shoes, without ever seeing it

When I the poet try to describe it –

> it loves us no more than before,
> and no less.

xix

I wanted to believe the body was right.

That even the rapist and molestor
carried seeds of rightness in some hidden chamber
of the wrong they did.

I wanted to believe the hard cock was right.
The soaring swaying tower of it, aiming the body forward.

I wanted the aching cunt to be right,
hidden, insistent, gnashing, hungering.

I wanted to believe the body could be trusted,
to believe need was a guide,
to praise desire
like a deity.

I wanted to believe the body was right,

but it was not.
(Neither was it wrong.)

xx

Sometimes this happens: ants find nests,
eat whole the just-fledged birds.

There is always one who begins the journey;
then another follows another
up the rough corpus of tree-trunk,
out the artery of branch,
down the vein of twig –
each moving as if blind and deaf
to everything but life's imperative,
each one so tiny I could crush it,
you could crush it, with a fingertip.

The ants in their speechless wisdom, which is hunger,
their hunger which is wisdom, which is
brainless, mindless, unrelenting wisdom,
travel the tree, one after another,
weave between the woven fibers of the nest,
swarm the frail dampness of the young,
and eat their fill.

And in this place, the birds had carried
each careful blade to the crotch of the tree;
they had rescued each piece of grass like a spear of star,
they had tugged them all into circles of nest,
forced the perfection of eggs from their bodies,
sat on the speckled sphere, warmed them like light –

and the new ones inside their shells
had somehow hammered their way out
with infant beaks, with life's imperative,
    emerging into the world all mouth, all want –

Life does not discriminate
Does not prefer itself over itself
Does not reject itself in favor of itself

Somewhere, today, a woman drowned
her five sons, one by one, in the bathtub.
The oldest was seven; he ran through the house;
    she chased him down, then held his head
    as long as she had to,
    under the unblinking skin of the water.
    Somewhere meanwhile a man
    stripped down his granddaughter.

Look. Do not avert your eyes. If you bend down
(as to the blood on the pavement), you will recognize
the grief in their hearts,

which also is your own.
You will recognize the heart,
wrong and right and small and blindly seeking like an ant,
eating where it can.

The vines of morning-glory are glorious,
    as they smother the roses.

(Life chooses all of us, and no one, in the same breath.
Life chooses God, which is itself, which is not as we thought.
Life chooses us, and the wrong/rightness of our thought,
and chooses against us.)

I grasp the daddy longlegs by one of its long legs
and the fly spun-around, cocooned, dead in its web,
and trail them like a galaxy on their sticky threads.
 Who knows the end of the story?
 Will I be able to love you enough?
 Will the flame in my body burn me
 or save me,
 are they the same thing?

I put my bare foot in the grass, and ants climb onto it.
The hairs on my leg sprout upward like grasses.
I reach myself out with love like a tendril, like an ant,
 like a bird with blades of star in my beak.

The end of the story has not been written yet